I0493095

The Entrepreneurial Brain

How The Entrepreneur's Brain Is Wired Differently From The Masses

Steven Imke

Copyright © 2016 by Steven Imke

All rights reserved. This book or any portion thereof may not be reproduced or used in any manner whatsoever without the express written permission of Steven Imke except for the use of brief quotations in a book review.

Produced in the United States of America

First Printing, 2016

ISBN-13: 978-1534702608
ISBN-10: 1534702601

KSI Enterprises
395 Scrub Oak Circle
Monument CO 80132

www.SteveBizBlog.com

About the Author

Steve's first foray into the world of small business came when he was an Invisible Fencing dealer. He operated this business on a part-time basis while remaining employed by a Fortune 500 company called Digital Equipment Corporation (DEC). While the Invisible Fencing business was not very successful for Steve, it was a valuable opportunity for him to learn important lessons about business in a relatively low-risk environment.

After ending his relationship with Invisible Fencing, he worked on a business plan for a new business idea and waited for the right opportunity to present itself. In 1994, DEC fell on hard times. Instead of bemoaning this turbulent economic tide, Steve capitalized on this opportunity. He quit his day job at DEC to found Horizon Interactive, a documentation and training company. In fact, Horizon Interactive became a vendor for DEC.

Over the next few years, Steve and his partners executed the business plan. The business grew to over $3 million in annual sales and opened offices in several states. Horizon Interactive's success drew the attention of Interleaf, a publicly held company out of Massachusetts. In 1999, Interleaf acquired Horizon Interactive.

As part of the acquisition, Steve was offered the position of VP of Operations for their services division. Under his leadership, Interleaf acquired two more businesses like

Horizon Interactive. The company grew the services side of the business from a combined $8 million in revenue to over $32 million in sales during the next two years.

In 2001, Interleaf was acquired by Broadvision, a California company during the height of the dot com era. Broadvision primarily acquired Interleaf for their XML engineers who worked on the product side of the business. Needing to divest himself from the services business, Steve and a former business partner acquired the assets of Interleaf's service business and started IC Interactive. They operated the business for a few more years until they sold it in 2003.

Being a serial entrepreneur, Steve has started and still operates three different businesses. One of his businesses is focused on real estate. The second one is focused on oil and gas. His third business is a company designed to help high net-worth investors understand the ins and outs of investing in oil and gas direct participation programs.

Steve has volunteered his time since 2003 as a mentor for SCORE, a local organization dedicated to helping entrepreneurs. He has acted as their Chapter Chairman for several years. He is also an advisory board member of his local Small Business Development Center (SBDC). In additions to his advisory role, he also acts as a counselor for the SBDC since 2003. In 2012, Steve acted as the interim director of SBDC while they conducted a national search for a permanent director. Currently, Steve is the Entrepreneurship Director at Pikes Peak Community College and writes a daily blog about small businesses.

Steve is a flaming dyslexic, which has its good points and bad points. Growing up, he remembers undergoing a board of education evaluation. When asked to draw a tree, Steve drew a series of concentric rings. When asked about his drawing, he said the rings were what you see when you cut down the tree and look at the stump. These rings tell the entire life story of the tree. The evaluator told his parents he was not normal. He should be more like the other kids and draw the tree from the side view.

However, rather than conform to the crowd, Steve embraced his out-of-the-box thinking as an asset. The upside of being dyslexic is exceptional spatial awareness and problems solving skills. Dyslexics develop these heightened skills since they are forced from an early age to compensate for things they do not do well.

Being a dyslexic in school prevented Steve from becoming a good reader. Even today, spelling and grammar are not his strong suits. Academically, Steve struggled in traditional schools. When he graduated from high school, he knew that a traditional classroom education was not for him so he joined the United States Coast Guard to learn a trade. Graduating near the top of his class in tech school, Steve realized that he learned by doing.

Steve tends to be an overly logical person. He likes to explore, document, and measure nearly every aspect of a project to find out what works and what does not. He has a propensity to focus on understanding why things are the way they are rather than how to duplicate what others have already done. Once Steve obtains a reasonable level of mastery in a specific subject area, he internalizes the knowledge and moves on to his next area of interest.

Everything of substance Steve knows about small business initially began by him reading books, listening to audiobooks, or watching others. He internalizes the salient points, then rolls up his sleeves and puts them into practice in his own business. Once Steve perfects a lesson, he makes it a point to document it and then share it with others. He calls these "Sea Stories," leveraging his old Coast Guard days. In addition to sharing his knowledge, this practice serves to further solidify his learning in his own mind while continuing to grow his knowledge base. In this way, Steve has codified over more than a decade's worth of his small business knowledge in the various books he has written.

This process has served Steve pretty well. By the time he was 42 years old, Steve had reached the point where he no longer needed to work for money. Passing this income milestone has not only allowed him the luxury to spend even more time to ponder and digest life's lessons, but also the freedom to tell it like it is without the fear of losing his job. He proudly wears jeans nearly every day. He also sports facial hair to remind himself and others that being a nonconformist and not subscribing to traditional viewpoints has its merits for entrepreneurs.

Steve constantly reads and listens to non-fiction audiobooks about politics or business related topics. He consumes current events from a huge basket of news sources every day so he can relate their messages in new and innovative ways. After internalizing a message and testing new theories, he shares his new-found wisdom with people willing to listen.

Since 2003, Steve has mentored and counseled thousands of fledgling entrepreneurs through his volunteer efforts with SCORE and SBDC. He has volunteered his expertise to help organizations like ARC, a program which helps individuals with developmental disabilities.

As cliché as it may sound, Steve is at the point in his life where it is all about using his skills and knowledge to help others to succeed. Steve never expects anything in return, but simply enjoys the appreciation he receives from the people he has helped and lives vicariously through their success. For Steve, sharing his knowledge is akin to the feeling a billionaire might have handing out $100 bills to random strangers on the street. He knows that by sharing some of the wisdom he has accumulated with clients, he can often make a positive difference in their lives. Steve is not particularly religious so helping entrepreneurs is his way of giving back and making a significant impact on the world around him.

Table of Contents

All Hat No Cattle

People that look like millionaires generally are not, according to the authors of the Millionaire Next Door. You might be surprised by the following millionaire facts.

About two-thirds of millionaires are self-employed. While self-employed people make up less than 20 percent of the workers in America, they account for almost 70 percent of the millionaires.

75 percent consider themselves to be entrepreneurs. The rest are self-employed professionals, such as doctors and accountants.

Many millionaire entrepreneurs operate non-glamorous businesses such as auctioneer, pest control, or paving businesses. They have an average household net worth of $3.7 million, but live in homes valued in the low 300k range.

They do not drive new or expensive automobiles. Most got to be millionaires because they didn't spend money on luxury items, choosing instead to invest about 20 percent of their household income.

While about 80 percent have an account with a brokerage firm, most make their own investment decisions.

Do you have what it takes to be a millionaire?

Copyright © 2016 Steven Imke

Cash Flow Quadrant

Robert Kiyosaki, the author of Rich Dad Poor Dad, uses a model he calls the Cash Flow Quadrant to explain the different ways income is generated.

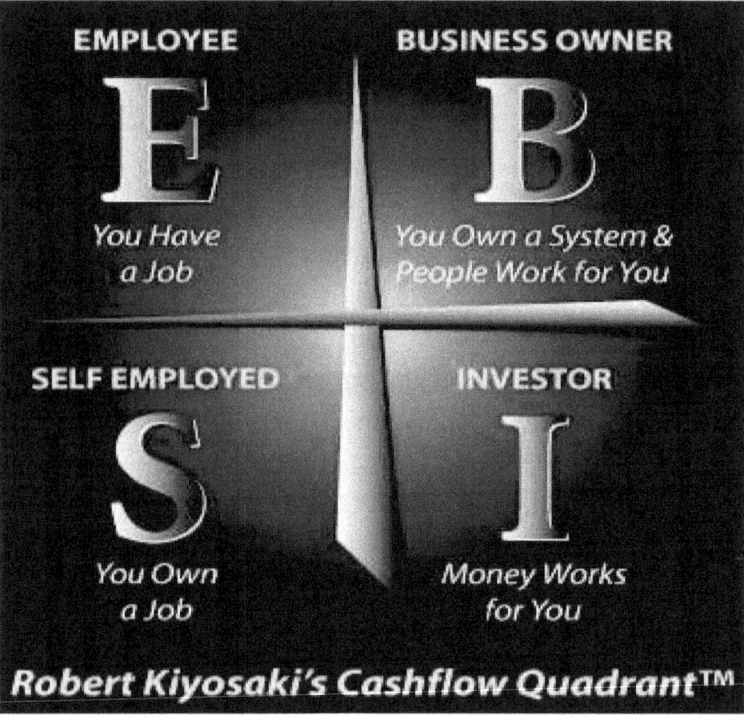

In the next few articles we will look at how income is generated in each of the four quadrants.

Of course income can be earned from a single quadrant or from a combination of quadrants, but we will look at each

Copyright © 2016 Steven Imke

quadrant separately in the coming days.

The four quadrants are named E, S, B, and I.

- E stands for Employee
- S for Self-Employed
- B for Business Owner and
- I for Investor.

If you divide the quadrant of income generation in half vertically, the left side contains quadrants E and S: Employee and Self-Employed. Here, your income is considered active income. That is, for the quadrants on the left side, you get paid for the number of hours you work. The two quadrants on the left are the playing field of the poor and the middle class.

On the right side of the quadrant are Business Owner and Investor, where your income is considered passive income. This means that you earn income from the labors of others. The two quadrants on the right are the playing field of the rich and financially independent.

Moving from the left side to the right requires capital, education, and a new mindset.

What side of the quadrant do you want to earn your income from?

Employee – Cash Flow Quadrant

When you are an Employee you know you will get a paycheck as long as you continue to work for the business, even if the business is not profitable. Earning a consistent wage each month is important when it comes to paying off debt, like home or car loans.

However, full-time employees get their income from this single source, their job, and if they lose their job they lose 100% of their income. They have to rely on unemployment to bridge any employment gaps.

Moreover, in terms of taxes, employees pay the highest percentage of their income. The more you earn as an employee the higher your tax bracket, and you have no options to reduce your income through deductions or tax credits.

Most Americans get their income from this quadrant.

How much of your income comes from wages earned as a employee?

Copyright © 2016 Steven Imke

Self-Employed – Cash Flow Quadrant

When you are Self-Employed, you own a job. The government also refers to this group as non-employer businesses, where the owner is the only employee.

When you are self-employed you trade one boss for several bosses, known as your customers.

While you have the flexibility to work the hours you want, you get paid only when you are under contract. The more you work, the more you get paid.

There are no paid vacations or holidays for the self-employed. Some self-employed individuals will derive income from several concurrent contracts, thereby achieving some level of diversification in their income.

However, many self-employed workers simply work for a previous employer or for a single customer as a contractor, and do not achieve any income diversification. In fact, many self-employed individuals have undertaken more income risk by becoming self-employed, with little if any additional compensation.

In terms of taxes, the self-employed person will have to pay the employer portion of FICA in addition to the employee portion, which is known as the self-employment tax on all taxable income.

However, many business expenses such as cell phones, travel, etc. can be paid for using pre-tax dollars, providing the self-employed opportunities to reduce their taxable income.

Savvy self-employed individuals price their services to adequately cover all their indirect expenses, including the additional employer-paid FICA share as well as any down-time experienced between projects.

How much of your income comes from self-employment, and is it priced properly?

Copyright © 2016 Steven Imke

Business Owner – Cash Flow Quadrant

Being a Business Owner is different from being self-employed in that as a business owner you hire employees to do the work. That is not to say that the business owner does not work in the business also, but it means that they are getting paid for their effort as an employee in the business PLUS for being an investor in the business.

Business owners can scale up their business, which is not possible for the self-employed. As the business hires more and more employees a fraction of each employee's bill-rate is the owner's return on investment for the start-up capital, as well as for undertaking the additional risk of business ownership.

As the business grows it generates more and more wealth for the owner. Like being self-employed, as a business owner you have several bosses or customers, but you are also the boss of your employees.

Business owners own systems that allow the owner to be absent for long periods and still generate income. Income diversification and taxes for business owners are similar to those of the self-employed.

However, if the business is an corporation (S-Corp or C-Corp), not all income is subjected to the combined 15.3% FICA contribution, as is the case for the self-employed. Wages from working in the business are subject to FICA.

The profit that is left after all expenses and salaries are paid is not subject to FICA.

Since being a business owner is where a majority of the rich make their money, what are your plans to generate more income from this quadrant?

Copyright © 2016 Steven Imke

Investor – Cash Flow Quadrant

The last quadrant is Investor. As an investor it is all about having your money work for you.

As an investor you can spread your investment money around to achieve greater income diversification, while lowing overall risk through less investment concentration.

There is an investment continuum related to taxes. On one end of the investment continuum is **interest income**, where income comes from sources like money markets, bonds and T-bills. **Ordinary dividends** (like you receive as a business owner) and short term capital gains are also on this same end of the continuum. All these investments do not receive any special tax treatment.

However, moving along the continuum, there are **qualified dividends** and **long-term capital gains** that benefit from special tax treatment. Rather than being taxed based on how much you make, these investment vehicles are taxed for most investors at a fixed 15% rate. One exception is for the ultra rich, who pay 20%, which is far less that most investors' marginal income tax rate.

Next on the continuum is **federal income tax-free interest income** known as municipal bonds.

Beyond that there is **income from real estate**, which allows for depreciation to lower taxable income. Further capital gains, which are normally taxed when the property is sold, can be deferred indefinitely using what is known as a 1031 exchange. This allows the investor to grow their assets without paying capital gains on each successive transaction.

Finally, there is **direct participation in oil and gas programs**. Investing in oil and gas programs allows the investor to write off most of his investment against other sources of income, such as wages. Also, a depletion allowance makes only 85% of the income subject to taxes. However, to play in this game, most investors need to be accredited. This means that they have a net worth in excess of one million dollars or earn in excess of $250,000.00 per year.

Since being an investor means your money works for you, what are your plans to generate more income from this quadrant?

Why the Rich Get Richer

People at the top of the wage scale are mostly employed in **thought** oriented jobs. The productivity of thought oriented jobs has been increasing at a greater pace than the productivity of workers at the bottom of the wage scale, who are mostly employed in **manual labor** oriented jobs.

With increasing productivity comes larger margins, and the ability for companies to pay workers more wages.

When a person's income level surpasses the point needed to maintain a comfortable lifestyle, surplus income can be directed away from consumption and poured into investments, growing ones net worth.

Basically, you begin to use your money earned from higher wages to make you more money through investments. Effectively, you create two income streams: one from wages and the other from your return on investments.

Once a person's net worth surpasses one million dollars or their wages exceed $250k per year, the threshold for being considered an Accredited Investor, a whole new world of investment opportunities becomes available.

These new investment opportunities often come with significant tax advantages to allow invested dollars to grow even faster. All this contributes to the fact that the income gap between the rich and poor is continuing to widen.

Copyright © 2016 Steven Imke

The first step for those people at the bottom of the wage scale that desire to become rich is to migrate their employment from manual labor oriented jobs to more thought oriented jobs to gain more income from wages.

This can be accomplished through either more education or by becoming self-employed. By resisting the urge to use the increased income for more consumption and instead investing it, the invested money will begin to grow their net worth.

In the end, income from wages is limited. You can only work so many hours per week. However, rich people accumulate wealth first through higher wages and then by making their money, which has no defined upper limit, work for them to make even more money. That is how the rich become richer while the working poor struggle to make ends meet.

Do you have a plan to become rich?

Understanding the Investment Risk Continuum

At some level all investors consider capital preservation when they make an investment. Capital preservation lies on one end of the risk continuum, while investments that put all your capital at risk generally offer the highest possibility of reward.

If your business invests in **inventory**, this represents a generally low risk scenario. The time frame between getting inventory and turning it back into cash is relatively short. Furthermore, if your inventory is not selling like you planned, you can discount it and preserve most of your capital. The upside of selling all the inventory is meager and the down side risk is also minimal. Investing in inventory is like buying a bond.

A more risky investment might be using your capital to develop and build new **production equipment**. The time horizon between investment and return is much longer than with the previous example involving inventory. Also, you run the risk of building a new product that no one wants. If this is the case you can sometimes sell the equipment for scrap, or try to repurpose it to preserve at least a small fraction of your capital investment. Investing in production equipment is like investing in public stocks.

Finally, on the far end of the continuum is investing in a

new **innovation or R&D**. Such an investment often takes years to get to market. Also, since most of the effort has no tangible assets, if the innovation fails the investment is generally a total loss. However, a successful innovation often has huge payoffs.   Investing in innovation is like being an entrepreneur and investing in a new start-up business.

In the end, generally, the more you try to preserve capital the less the ultimate payoff will be.

Where do your investments fit on the risk continuum?

What an Ear of Corn Can Teach Us

If you were given an ear of corn today you would have a few options. You could eat the ear of corn and receive nourishment today. You could forgo the nourishment from the corn today and save/horde the ear for its seeds, which you could sell or plant at a later date. You could forgo the nourishment from the corn today and plant the seeds and have lots of corn plants with hundreds of ears of corn by this time next year. Or you could combine the options: eat some of the corn, save some of it, and wait and plant some.

The prevailing culture in American is one of instant gratification, which translates into our business culture. Most Americans if given the ear of corn would simply eat it. But how hard would it be to eat most of of the corn today and save just a few kernels so you could plant them next year?

On average, a single ear of corn has about 800 kernels. Would you really miss the nourishment from not eating a few of the seeds? After all, an investment of saving just a one seed from consumption could by next year grow an entire plant with multiple ears from each kernel you didn't eat today.

Many business owners leach every dollar of profit to support a consumption-oriented lifestyle for themselves today. They live in "daylight compartments" and consume all that their businesses produce. Life is good in the short term, since they ate their entire ear of corn. However, these businesses will soon become part of the statistics on business failure.

By contrast, a person who is willing to deny themselves the satisfaction of eating the entire ear of corn today, and start by just keeping a few kernels for seed stock to plant next year, will in only a year or two never be wanting for corn ever again. And it all started with saving just a few seeds from the first ear.

Too many business owners do not make the needed investments in their businesses to allow them to grow.

Are you guilty of taking too much from your business and not investing in its future?

Business Investing 101

For individuals, your labor alone will never make you rich. Working harder and longer may create a small boost in income, but you will never become truly rich this way.

To become truly rich requires that you control consumption and invest your excess capital to make your money work for you. The same is true with business.

Using a company's free cash to buy more inventory is like working longer and harder at your job. It might allow you to bring in a little more money, but it will never make the company grow rich.

However, investing the free cash in R&D efforts to develop a new product line can make a company grow and become rich.

Do you understand your investment strategy?

Can Profits Be Too High?

Statistically, an Angel Investor or a venture capital firm that invests in ten different companies may see one of the companies take off and exceed a return of 1,000%, or ten times the investment. Two of the companies will do just okay and do little more than break even, while the remaining seven investments will lose most if not all the invested capital. At some point the return from the one successful investment has to not only cover the loss of the seven investments that went bust, but also return a portfolio profit to the investor.

Entrepreneurs are angel investors of sorts, with an investment portfolio of one company. From the other side, the non-investor looks at the one successful investment and says the investor or successful entrepreneur is profiting way too much.

They believe that excessive profit is somehow inherently unfair, and that there must be a way to take some of that profit from the investor and redistribute it to the working class through higher wages or higher taxes. They do not see the money that the angel investor invested in the seven companies that were a total loss.

Such thinking is pervasive among the vast majority of working class American citizens, who do not understand how investing in a small business really works. Ultimately this thinking leads to the image of a fat, cigar smoking

Copyright © 2016 Steven Imke

investor making huge sums of money at the expense of the lowly workers, who toil endlessly to make the investor rich while they struggle to put food on the table for their families.

Nothing could be further from the truth, since the investor paid the salary of the workers out of his invested funds. When the investment failed, the investor lost his money and now has nothing to show for it. Except for, perhaps, an expensive lesson in business.

The thinking that investors are taking advantage of workers undermines the very investments in small business ventures that pay many workers' salaries.

Even when an investment spawns a successful business, its profit window can be limited. Google makes a lot of money today, but for how long? Google supplanted Yahoo, which supplanted AOL, which supplanted Prodigy. Prodigy is now out of business.

Investors often have to make their investment return in a short time, known as the "Return to Exit". In the short term it may look like investors earn a huge return, but considering overall success rates and short profit windows, returns are often very similar to the market as a whole. It is simply unfair to look a single year and say that investors' returns are unfairly large.

Is your view of small business investments realistic?

Copyright © 2016 Steven Imke

Angel Investors

The term "Angel Investor" comes from the the theater, where a wealthy investor often came to the rescue and provided the money necessary to bring a play into production.

Angel investors are generally entrepreneurs that had a profitable exit event and were able to cash in on their companies' successes.

Many of these successful entrepreneurs feel they have the "Midas Touch" and can repeat their success as an investor vs. as a business owner. Rather than investing in a single business like the one they once owned, they look to diversify their portfolio by investing in several businesses.

Most successful entrepreneurs get personal satisfaction learning how to conquer a specific industry. Angel Investors are no different, but they often invest in ventures that are somewhat foreign to them.

While many of the business lessons they learned can apply to any business, each industry has its unique set of challenges to success. This mismatch often leads to creative tension between founders and the Angel Investor(s), leading many founders to try to do it alone.

That being said, Angel Investments are often what I would call smart money, in that the Angels often have expertise and connections that the fledgling business entity desperately needs.

According to data gathered by Southern California's "Tech Coast Angels", only 1 in 72 entrepreneurs looking for an Angel Investor were successful in obtaining any funding.

So how does a founder locate an Angel Investor? Most communities have organizations made up of successful entrepreneurs looking to invest in the next home-run company. Your local public library likely has a list of these organizations. Absent that, there is the Angel Capital Association that can help connect founders to Angel Investors.

Can your business benefit from an investment from an Angel Investor?

An Entrepreneur's Perspective on Education and Success

As you might imagine I have the occasion to speak to lots of successful business people and spend much of my time trying to understand what attributes make for a successful entrepreneur.

One difference I see is how non-entrepreneurs and entrepreneurs approach education. The vast majority of my friends that have successful jobs working for large corporations or for the government, we'll call then non-entrepreneurs, credit their success to college educations. which they say helped launch them on their successful career trajectories.

By contrast, a much larger percentage of my friends that are entrepreneurs never finished college or say they never really used what they learned in college.

I don't mean to imply that entrepreneurs have not benefited from a college education. My entrepreneur friends simply view education differently. To be more specific, entrepreneurs value the acquisition of specific kernels of knowledge over a general education.

When asked, my entrepreneur friends are never at a loss to come up with a list of areas of interest they want to gain a greater understanding of, or to share the latest topic they

Copyright © 2016 Steven Imke

just researched.

Another less obvious but tangential difference is related to how each group views success.

When I share my business story with non-entrepreneurs the questions I get most often are more related to "what did you DO to become successful", as if it was a single event they could emulate that led to my business success.

By contrast, similar discussions with entrepreneurs tend to focus on investments in ourselves, such as how did you identify and acquire the knowledge that led to your successes?

Non-entrepreneurs tend to focus on what they have to "do" to become successful, while entrepreneurs tend to focus on what they need to "be" to become successful.

How do you think about education and success?

Are You Reading This?

A recent Pew Research Center report showed that Americans today really don't feel much pressure to keep up with news and public issues. In fact, only 37% of Americans think that it is important to keep abreast of current events shaping U.S. and world politics.

While my sons, who are in their 20s and 30s, might occasionally ask me questions like "why are gas prices dropping?", they do not regularly watch TV news, read a newspaper, or even use the internet or social media to keep up with news and public issues. In fact, only one in five Americans say it is part of their civic duty as a voting American to stay informed.

Younger Americans, who have access to an unprecedented amount of information on smart phones, tablets, internet, etc., feel even less obligated to understand the issues facing our country.

Civic virtue is in serious decline, especially with the younger generation. I believe that as a country that is a constitutionally limited representative democratic republic, every American, rich or poor, young or old, has the civic duty to keep up with news and public issues that affect us all, so long as they have the right to vote.

Personally, I take every opportunity to corner my adult children and talk to them about pressing issues of the day. I

Copyright © 2016 Steven Imke

do my best to represent both sides of the issues when talking to them, but often express my exasperation with certain issues about which I feel particularly strongly.

With today's 24/7 news cycle, there is no excuse for an absence of information. There is only the eroding sense of duty felt by Americans to remain informed.

If you are reading this story today, share the message with your friends and make a commitment to talk to your children tonight and instill in them the value that we as Americans have to remain actively engaged in the news and public issues affecting us all.

Copyright © 2016 Steven Imke

The Mind of the Entrepreneur Series

Everyone's belief system is shaped by the company they keep. Entrepreneurs are no different in that regard. The differences in beliefs comes from the village of advisers people use.

For example, fat people who hang around other fat people will not be exposed to better eating habits, will be exposed to negative thinking about being overweight, and will likely continue to struggle with weight issues. However, a fat person that hangs around with thin people will be exposed to healthier eating habits, be encouraged to lose weight with positive "can do" messages, and stand a good chance of losing weight.

That said, based on the company they keep, the ways entrepreneurs and the wealthy think about things like money, investing, and work can be quite different from the the thinking of the general public. The next few stories in this eBook we compare and contrast the general narrative of the masses with the belief systems of successful entrepreneurs and the wealthy so you can see what you are missing by hanging out with the wrong crowd.

What kind of people are in your village of advisers?

Work for a Wage vs. Creative Thinking

Most people, when they think about money, think money is what you get when you sell your time. For example, they trade a 40 hour work week for a wage.

Entrepreneurs know that money is generated by identifying problems and selling solutions. They understand that money is not earned through ones labor but through ones creative thinking.

How do you think about money?

Solitary Hard Work vs. Leverage

Most people think that to create personal wealth requires hard work. They work hard from from 9-5 and get paid for their results.

Consider the construction worker or waitress who engages in hard physical labor for their wages. Furthermore, they believe that building wealth is a solitary effort and they crave recognition for the efforts they contribute.

Entrepreneurs know that leverage, not hard work, is what creates wealth. They enlist the help of people in their personal network who have specialized skills, allowing each to work less and achieve greater combined results. It is not recognition that drives entrepreneurs, but results. They will readily exchange credit for money.

Entrepreneurs take tasks, break them into their component steps, and then outsource any fungible steps. They use tools like Upwork.com, Frelancer.com or Guru.com to send pieces of the work to offshore specialists who can do them faster and at a lower cost.

Do you view work as a solitary effort or as a team effort to leverage expertise?

Money is for Spending vs. Investing

Most people believe that money is meant to be spent for articles of instant gratification as a reward for their efforts. These same people usually live beyond their means and fund their lifestyle with debt. They also spend their leisure time in activities that have no real value, such as watching sports or reading novels.

Entrepreneurs know that to be successful one needs to keep personal spending and bad debt low. They spend their leisure time reading self help or business related books, volunteer and build personal networks, or watch the news to keep up with current events.

In their book The Millionaire Next Door Thomas Stanley and William Danko interviewed successful and wealthy individuals and discovered that they live well below their means.

Entrepreneurs and millionaires believe in delayed gratification and know that the key to financial security requires investment in both time and money.

Do you see money as a reward that should be spent today or as something saved and invested for financial freedom tomorrow?

No Network vs. Large Network

Most people underestimate the power of referrals, while entrepreneurs know that referral marketing creates wealth.

They participate on panels, non-profit boards, and other functions, most often for free and without any expectation of a direct return.

However, the results of their efforts give them large personal networks that return dividends in many unexpected ways.

With the exception of enlisting in the Coast Guard, I have never applied for a job. I try to treat everyone well and have created a network that understands my worth. Every employment and investment opportunity has come to me via personal referrals from my network.

How big is your referral network?

Pleasure vs. Money Making Activities

Most people when not working are engaged in pleasure-focused activities, such as watching TV. Many of my friends can tell you a baseball player's batting average, can handicap college basketball teams during March madness, or can tell you the movies that featured any particular actor.

Entrepreneurs are engaged in money making activities. A love of real estate manifests itself in property speculation, a love of fine art in art collections, a love of numbers in trading stocks, or a love of people in networking.

The difference is that much of an entrepreneurs' leisure activity is rooted in their ability to convert their activities into something in which they can get some form of return.

How do you spend your leisure time?

Safe vs. Calculated Risk

Most people work hard for their money. Therefore, when it comes to investing their hard earned money, they tend to play it very safe and conservative.

Entrepreneurs know that money doesn't not come from work but from ideas and ones personal knowledge. They know that even if they lost all their money in a series of bad investments they still retain the capacity to earn it back with their knowledge. They treat investing like a science, testing and measuring results, and are willing to take calculated risks based on potential rewards.

How do you view investing?

Copyright © 2016 Steven Imke

Linear vs. Non-Linear Thinking

Most people think in a very linear fashion. When they discover a potentially promising investment they look at their income and expenses and say "I just can't afford it", and pass up many good deals.

Entrepreneurs are not constrained by money and think more non-linearly. When exposed to a promising investment they look at its risks and potential returns and say "Is it worth it?". If the answer is yes they move on it.

If they are short of funds they compile their reasoning and pitch the idea to debt or equity partners. If after their pitch no one buys their reasoning, perhaps it was not a good idea.

Is your thinking more linear or non-linear?

Copyright © 2016 Steven Imke

Test Smart or Street Smart

Most people think since they were perhaps not very good in school they are just not smart enough to be an entrepreneur. They associate being smart only with a high intelligence quotient or IQ.

IQ is a measure of how one does on tests or more specifically how well a person can memorize and recall information. Performing poorly in academic settings has little or no bearing on ones potential success as a entrepreneur.

In most academic settings you are presented with the lesson's material and then given a test to determine how much of the information you can recall and given a grade.

Today the world is quite different with respect to IQ. Most of us have 24/7 access to the internet. Given any question to which we do not have an immediate response we can use a search engine like Google to find the answer in milliseconds.

Some people are good at memorizing facts, are successful in academic situations, and are test smart. Some have physical prowess, make good athletes, and are smart physically. Some have a capacity to discern rhythm, tone, and timbre, and are music smart. Some are good at making network connections and are people smart.

Howard Gardner (howardgardner.com) lists <u>nine types of smarts</u>.

1. Naturalist Intelligence ("Nature Smart")
2. Musical Intelligence ("Musical Smart")
3. Logical-Mathematical Intelligence (Number/Reasoning Smart)
4. Existential Intelligence (Human Existence Smart)
5. Interpersonal Intelligence (People Smart")
6. Bodily-Kinesthetic Intelligence ("Body Smart")
7. Linguistic Intelligence (Word Smart)
8. Intra-personal Intelligence (Self Smart")
9. Spatial Intelligence ("Picture Smart")

In the end the question is not "How smart are you?" but "How are you smart?".

The Power Of Leverage

Most serious investors understand the power of leverage. When it comes to investing in stocks many sophisticated investors have a margin account with their broker that allows them to pledge their securities as collateral for the ability to borrow money (usually up to half the portfolio's value) from their broker to invest more than the value of their portfolio.

A person with $100k in stocks can invest $150k, $50k being borrowed. In this way they can add to their actual $100 portfolio value to achieve greater rewards than the $100k could alone.

I own an investment, a restaurant, that pays a 7.5% annual return. I put down 40% of my own cash and borrowed the other 60% from a lender at 6%.

On my 40% I make a 7.5% return, plus I pocket an additional 1.5% (7.5% minus 6%) return on the 60% of the borrowed money, making the overall return of 9.75%.

Therefore, for taking on the addition of what I would say is a very minimal increased level of risk, I use leverage (the bank's money) to maximize my returns. As business owners, we also want to use leverage whenever possible to extend our returns.

Do you use leverage to maximize your business returns?

Copyright © 2016 Steven Imke

Money = Personal Freedom

I have often stated that most people are not really motivated by money itself. Rather, I say that money is just a means to achieve social and professional standing, also known as status.

I would add to that idea that the accumulation of wealth, most often accomplished through business ownership, also leads to personal freedom. The freedom to not rely on the government, the freedom to get out of bad or unpleasant economic situations, the freedom to fight oppression, etc.

Are you on a path to personal freedom?

Knowledge Trumps Money

If money is your hope for independence, you will never have it.

The only real security that a man can have in this world is a reserve of knowledge, experience and ability.

The saying "easy come easy go" refers to the fact that having money without knowledge means that you will soon be separated from your money.

You can lose all your money, but you can never lose the knowledge and skills you obtain during your life.

With knowledge and experience you can rebuild your wealth if it is lost.

Do you have the knowledge, experience, and skill to rebuild your wealth if you lost all your money?

Optimism: Your Psychological Insulator

Most people operate from a fear based mentality and are cynical about new ideas. After all, if you don't expect much you will not be disappointed, right?

Entrepreneurs do not succumb to fear based thinking and are optimistic by nature. Entrepreneurs think everything they touch will turn to gold. Even when they experience failure they believe the next idea will succeed.

Optimism is a psychological insulator that keeps entrepreneurs moving forward even in the face of failure.

Are you optimistic about your future?

Time to Build a Ship

The other day I saw an interesting quote that got me thinking.

"Some people spend their entire life waiting for their ship to come in, not realizing that they are standing in an airport."

The concept of waiting for a ship to come in is rooted in the idea that someone else is driving. Waiting is based on hope and not personal action.

Rather than eat right and exercise to lose weight and become more healthy, many people are waiting for a pill (their ship to come in) that will solve all their problems.

They don't plan for retirement because the government and the social security system (their ship) will take care of them.

Entrepreneurs do not wait for things to happen. They are self-reliant and make things happen. They build their own ships.

Are you waiting for your ship to come in, or are you making plans to build your own ship?

Exposing Yourself

The Civil Rights Act of 1964 was an attempt to provide equal rights for black Americans. It expressly prohibited discrimination in voting, education, and public facilities. Although fraught with lots of implementation issues, integration in schools changed many people's mindset about other races.

It is human nature to like "like-minded people". We often erect artificial barriers to segregate "non-like minded people" to keep them out of our network circles.

When you understand that our views of the world and how we see opportunities are colored by the company we keep, you can see that by not venturing outside your village of friends leads to group think, and prevents exposure to new ideas.

In the book *Who Owns the Ice House*, by Clifton Taulbert and Garry Schoeniger, Uncle Cleve, a black man living in the Mississippi delta in the 1950's, refused to be subjected to group think. Rather than work in the cotton fields like everyone else, he chose to break out and became an entrepreneur: an ice distributor.

Being exposed to rich white people delivering ice in the 1950's he became exposed to new idea and ways of thinking. He learned that there were no local garages to service the rich people's new cars so Uncle Cleve opened a garage. Had Uncle Cleve not expanded his personal network he never would have been exposed to the need for a local garage.

Since entrepreneurs know that ideas and knowledge are the real drivers of success, they know that group think is their mortal enemy.

Rather then be insulated from new ideas, entrepreneurs look for every opportunity to connect with people outside their clique.

What are you doing to reach out and expose yourself to new people and ideas?

Seed Money

It is always good to have some investment funds so you have the ability to execute when you see a good deal.

One of my boys bought his motorcycle with cash after he bought a Ford Ranger with a blown engine the owner could not afford to fix. He bought the truck for $500 and put in a used but working engine for $1,000. For a case of beer and some pizza he had a few friends help him swap out the old engine with the working engine over a weekend. The following week he sold the truck for $4,500 and made a cool $3,000 for a weekend's work.

Had he not had a small investment fund, worth less then $2,000 at the time, he would have had to pass on the deal and miss out on making $3,000 with a very limited amount of effort or risk.

In another story a client of mine wanted to buy into a gym franchise but didn't have the money. He looked around for a way to make a quick buck. He contacted the college where he went to school and offered to sell them spirit towels they could use as a promotional giveaway at sporting events.

When they agreed he contacted a manufacturer in China and placed an order for tens of thousands of spirit towels for a small down payment. When the order arrived, he sold the lot to the college, paid off the remaining invoice and pocketed a tidy profit, which he used to cover his franchise deposit.

The take away is that you need to have the discipline to not buy everything you want. You need to squirrel away a few dollars here and there to create a small investment fund. This will allow you to take advantage of investment deals that help you to grow your fund when they come your way.

Do you have the seed money to act as leverage if you are presented with a fantastic investment opportunity?

Copyright © 2016 Steven Imke

Obsession is Not a Dirty Word

When you think of obsession does the idea strike a negative chord in your mind? For many, being obsessed is something to be avoided. Not so with entrepreneurs, who view obsession as a game they love to play.

Personally, I'm always obsessed with something new. When I find something I enjoy I go all in for a time to learn all I can about the topic. Once I master it, or at least reach a minimal level proficiency where there is a significant point of diminishing returns, I codify my experience and move on to my next obsession.

As a kid growing up in New England I wanted to hunt. However, the relativity confined spaces of my environment made it hard to find enough open ground to hunt with a gun, so I took up bow hunting. Obsessed with the idea of bow hunting, that summer I bought my first bow. I practiced every day for months and soon outgrew my first bow. I bought a better, more powerful bow, and continued to practice with it until I got pretty good. I would fill a gallon milk jug with sand, suspend it from a rope, and get it swinging in front of a back stop. Then I would take aim and practice hitting a moving object.

By the time hunting season came around that fall I was ready to decimate the local squirrel population. With my bounty of squirrels and other small game animals I moved on to my next obsession, taxidermy. I had realized I could not only enjoy eating the game I killed, but could make a few bucks mounting the animals and selling them to friends.

When I discovered ways that I could turn my obsessions into something I could make some money with, it added an even greater level of excitement to the game.

Many non-entrepreneurs see entrepreneurs as obsessed with success and making money, while they prefer instead to simply turn on the TV to entertain themselves. Being obsessed with something is the core of the entrepreneurial mindset.

Do you have an obsession? How can you turn your obsession into a way to make money?

The Middle Class Sputnik Moment

When agrarian society faded in favor of the more profitable industrial era, no matter how hard you worked as a farmer or how hard the farming industry tried to preserve itself the tide of change could not be turned.

By the same logic, no matter how hard we try to reestablish a middle class based on industrial era jobs, the internet and cheap offshore labor has created a tide no amount of hope and legislation can hold back.

Just as the farmer had to accept the change and adapt, so too does the middle class. The mind set of middle class workers who are employed in laborer-oriented professions and only think about working for others need to adapt, just like the farmers had to.

Rather than work harder at their job and hope their contributions are recognized and rewarded with higher wages, the middle class worker of the future needs to rethink the game as the rules are changing.

My dad worked nearly his entire adult life for one company. Today, according the a 2014 Bureau of Labor Statistics report, the median number of years a worker spends with one employer is just 4.6 years and going down.

The idea of career and wage growth over time within a company is no longer valid. The idea of climbing the

Copyright © 2016 Steven Imke

corporate ladder rung by rung has been rewritten.

Furthermore, more companies are reducing the number of hours workers can work to keep employees under mandated benefit thresholds.

Jim Clifton, the CEO of Gallup, said recently that the percent of full-time jobs in this country as a percent of the adult population "is the worst it's been in 30 years."

The methods of earning an income are changing and workers need to adapt by embracing a more entrepreneurial way of thinking if they want to survive financially.

Rather than derive all their income from a single job, middle class workers need to consider earning income from additional sources. They need to look for everyday problems they can solve. That is what it will take to transform the middle class.

While labor is limited by available time, earnings from innovation are not limited. This is our "Sputnik moment".

Firms like flooring giant Shaw Industries pared down their work force from 28,000 to 23,000 during the 2008 recession. Since then, with heavy investments in robotics and mechanization, they have rebuilt their revenue to near prerecession levels. While the company has boosted wages for some of its master mechanics, it feels no pressure to increase wages for the unskilled positions it still retains.

It is time to choose: either derive more income from multiple sources, or wait in vain for someone to rescue you.

With more labor-saving innovations being introduced into the market every day there is less and less need for jobs that simply provide labor. More laborers chasing fewer and fewer jobs means companies can get away with paying lower wages.

Do you think like an entrepreneur and pursue multiple sources of income?

Think Like an Entrepreneur

Most people think people become wealthy because they are lucky, had good fortune, or had some social advantage in life. They believe that everyone is their brother's keeper and that the ones who are fortunate to have money should share it with the less fortunate.

As I see it, we live in a free market society. Everyone has the opportunity to become wealthy if they think like an entrepreneur. Many successful company founders started with only a few hundred dollars and never had any advantages growing up that led to their success. In fact, many had to overcome great obstacles to achieve their success.

While most wealthy people are charitable with their money, they give for the sake of giving because it makes them feel good and not because of any moral code or pressure to do so. In fact, when forced to give, many people object and find ways to shelter their money. Furthermore, giving people unearned income robs them of the satisfaction they would get from obtaining money through their own achievements. Forced redistribution of wealth not only creates resistance from the wealthy, it creates psychological destruction in the recipient.

What are you going to do to help the less fortunate to think more like a entrepreneurs, rather than make them dependent on policies that redistribute wealth?

How to Exit the Rat Race

Robert Kiyosaki said it best:

"Most people are stuck between fear and greed, which makes them slaves to a job."

They live paycheck to paycheck and live in fear of losing their job and not being able to support their lifestyle. When they receive windfall income, such as a tax return or a raise, greed kicks in and they think of ways to spend it rather then save and invest the money.

Being able to manage money is a key attribute to entrepreneurship. Succumbing to greed will only keep you harnessed to the cycles of fear and greed and prevent you from breaking free of the rat race.

I'm pretty confident that if you took all the money in the world and distributed it evenly among every human it would not be long before all the money was back in the hands of the rich, because they understand how to manage money.

To become emancipated from the slavery of a job and achieve a level of financial freedom you have to first become moneywise and control your tendency to spend money as fast as you get it.

It starts with a rainy day fund. Without a rainy day fund, cash flow hiccups force you to either take on more debt or miss other payments, destroying your credit and making matters worse.

According to a CNBC article one-third of all Americans have no rainy day fund and are a hairsbreadth away from financial ruin.

Even with a small rainy day fund established you can now afford to invest in quick return opportunities that will allow you to build your wealth. As the fund grows you can afford to take some of the reserve funds and make more lucrative longer term investments to begin to grow your wealth.

Are you like most people, living paycheck to paycheck?

What are you doing to become a better money manager and become more financially independent?

Using Your Peripheral Vision to Spot Opportunities

I have a year and a half year old pedigree German Shepherd. He is a pretty good looking male with a great temperament towards people and other dogs. This temperament is rare among many German Shepherds because they are often good with people, but less so with other dogs.

A friend and colleague of mine also has a good looking and pedigree female German Shepherd with a very sweet temperament. A few months ago we decided to breed them and were blessed with six adorable puppies.

The other day I saw an article about a university in the UK that used puppies to relieve their students' stress during finals. This got me thinking. Entrepreneurs develop their peripheral vision to see things that many others do not.

My friend with the female German Shepherd has been going though a rough patch for the past few years. He has suffered the loss of a great paying job, a nasty divorce, health issues, and a huge wildfire that burned down nearly the his entire community. However, ever since the puppies were born a few weeks ago, his mood has taken a remarkable upward turn.

By itself I might not have noticed his transformation.

However, after reading the article published by the university in the UK and reflecting upon the situation, it is very clear that exposure to a puppy can transform even the most ill tempered curmudgeon or stressed out person into a real softy.

People just love babies and pets. Think about the joy you could bring to folks living in an independent living facility by exposing them to puppies.

In my grandfather and father's final days, they most look forward to the days that the dog lady would show up. Although the dogs she brought were usually older service dogs, the entire experience could have been amplified if she came with cute and adorable puppies.

My wife often says babies and puppies have to be cute and adorable so people will agree to have them and raise them. This is because they all grow up to become pain-in-the-ass teenagers and dogs that try your patience.

Since most of the residents in an independent living facility are in their twilight years, they know they will never have the chance to have a puppy of their own again. Exposing these puppies to the residents would not only bring the elderly joy, it would help to socialize the puppies to human contact.

In addition, it would give the puppies boundless amounts of love and human affection from gentle and kind people. It could also bring in donations if you used a tip jar to defray the expense of raising the puppies until they are ready for adoption.

Entrepreneurs expose themselves to lots of ideas and then use their peripheral vision to spot opportunities that others miss.

Do you use your peripheral vision to spot opportunities?

Academic Education Overrated?

Many successful entrepreneurs know that being successful is not about academic education. Instead they know that being successful is about focus and persistence.

Many successful entrepreneurs are high school and college dropouts. They quit school because they didn't see the purpose of what they were learning.

Many school curriculums are too narrow or too broad in scope. They are also outdated and lack the proper data to teach what it takes to be successful. Most teachers and professors went to college and upon graduation spent the next 40 years teaching what they learned. They have no idea what it takes to be a successful entrepreneur.

While many successful entrepreneurs have a formal education, few credit their success to what they learned in school. Being a successful entrepreneur is less about academic education and more about being focused. You need to do what it takes to achieve your goals.

Are you banking on academic achievement to make you a successful entrepreneur or are you ready to roll up your sleeves and just do it?

Copyright © 2016 Steven Imke

Tax Avoidance

As I write this, the <u>federal debt</u> is passing through the eighteen trillion threshold, but what does that have to do with me? It is not my debt. Someone else will pay it. Even if I owe a share, there are over three hundred million people in America and my share is not too much, right?

That is how most people think about the fiscal debt problem. As an abstract concept, it is hard to grasp unless you have the curiosity to do a little more research. In an effort to calculate the real impact of the national debt, let's take the total national debt figure and divide it by the number of US tax payers. After doing this calculation, the result is each tax payer owes $154,000.

Now imagine having $154,000 in credit card debt and nothing to show for it. Now you can begin to see the extent of the problem. With the debt per taxpayer as high as it is, the government will have no other option except to raise taxes on middle and high income earners at some point in the near future.

It may be framed under a pretense of patriotism, but it will be just another excuse to extract money from the private sector to pay for a bloated government. Taxes may not be restricted to just income taxes, but may come from higher sales taxes; additional excise taxes commonly applied to specific products like cigarettes and gas; and higher inheritance or ownership transfer taxes. They may even

Copyright © 2016 Steven Imke

come in even more obscure ways to disguise the tax and fool the average persons by imposing tariffs or duties on imports which makes products more expensive for the consumer while generating revenue for the government.

Higher taxes, in what ever form, will make it difficult for citizens to preserve their standard of living. As the private sector wealth shrinks, economic activity will slow, resulting in fewer new small businesses and smaller wage increases for employees. Therefore, these individuals will be squeezed from both ends (taxes and wages).

This is one of the key reasons why the middle class is shrinking. While it may be difficult to avoid many taxes, exposure to income taxes can be reduced. How do you inoculate yourself today to reduce your exposure to the inevitable storm that is coming? One way is to become an entrepreneur.

As an entrepreneur, you have business expenses that allow you to pay for things with pretax dollars. For example, let's look at how much a $100 a month cell phone for business really costs when you use pre-tax dollars vs. when you don't. If you use pre-tax dollars, the business cell phone really only costs $100 per month. However, if you use post-tax dollars, you have to figure in how much tax you need to pay in addition to the $100. If your total accumulated federal and state income tax rate is 50%, then you have to earn $200 of pre-tax income to net $100 after taxes, making the cell phone's real cost $200 per month.

Copyright © 2016 Steven Imke

Additionally, while the marginal tax rate may go up, earning more income will help to sustain your standard of living. According to the 2013 tax census, the median net worth at retirement for employees is just over $300,000. By contrast, the median net worth of someone that is self employed is $2,100,000.

We are all on the deck of the Titanic. Most of the passengers are continuing to sing and dance, ignoring the signs that the ship is sinking.

Are you part of masses living in denial until it is too late or are you making plans to survive?

www.ingramcontent.com/pod-product-compliance
Lightning Source LLC
Chambersburg PA
CBHW060420190526
45169CB00002B/979